Dyslexia

A Staff Development Handbook

Colin Tyre

Dedicated to the late Peter Young

First published in 1994
Revised edition published in 1998

ISBN 1 898873 06 2

Published by QEd, The Rom Building, Eastern Avenue, Lichfield, Staffs. WS13 6RN

Further copies of this book may be obtained from:
QEd, The Rom Building, Eastern Avenue, Lichfield, Staffs. WS13 6RN

Typeset in Times New Roman and printed in the UK by Stowes (Stoke-on-Trent).

Contents

Introduction

This publication is based upon a series of one-day courses given by Colin Tyre. Its aim is to provide a framework within which teachers can develop an understanding of dyslexia or specific learning difficulties in acquiring written language skills.

Reading is enjoyable, informative, useful and, in our culture, essential. The sudden realization that they are reading hits some children with all the force of a 'Eureka!' experience. When our children learn to read, we, as parents and teachers, are both proud for them and relieved that they have achieved this milestone in their development. When our children fail to learn to read, and fail to respond to teachers' specialist help, we suspect their eyesight, their hearing, their mental abilities, their heredity, ourselves and the way they have been brought up. Of all the hundreds of things we may want for children to achieve, socially, athletically, musically, intellectually, or in any other way, reading is an achievement which looms large in our hopes.

Reading, it was once suggested, will become less important in the 'electronic global village' into which children are growing. Nothing can be further from the truth. Developments in new and advanced technologies have simply accelerated the demands for higher levels of literacy and numeracy. Unfortunately, the signs abound that not only are we failing to keep up with demand, we are falling further behind. I was recently shown the results of first-term screening in a ten-form-entry comprehensive school. Seventy children (21 per cent) of this first year had reading ages below the age of nine and many of these below the age of eight.

If a basic level of literacy and articulateness is not attained by the age of seven, it becomes very difficult to achieve competence in any other learning, much of which relies on the ability to read, to discuss and to record in writing. The effects may persist, and become increasingly disadvantageous, throughout the primary stage and beyond. It is often the case that children of normal intelligence who have reading difficulties at the end of the primary phase are seriously underachieving at 16.

Children differ greatly in their preschool experience in that 'some will have books read to them and may have begun to read, while others have not'. Meeting the National Curriculum aims and objectives in schools where the large majority of children read or are ready to read, will pose few problems. In schools with less favoured intakes, unless the curriculum can respond to the literacy and numeracy needs of disadvantaged children, the grim picture of functional illiteracy in school leavers will continue.

'For too long, too many primary school teachers have been prevented from giving literacy and numeracy the attention they deserve because the National Curriculum has lacked the very clear focus on the basics which is crucial in primary education. As a result, literacy and numeracy have been too often subsumed into other subjects and it is no surprise that so many pupils leave primary school ill-equipped in the 3Rs.'

David Blunkett, Education and Employment Secretary

Many solutions for raising the national literacy standards are outside the influence of individual teachers. However, in our work in schools, many teachers report of their sketchy training in the teaching of written language skills. The preparation for the teaching of reading was cursory and particularly poor concerning assessment despite the advice given by Sir Alan Bullock as early as 1975 on initial training.

If reading standards are to improve, it is necessary that *all* teachers have sufficient knowledge to be able to differentiate their teaching so that *all* children realize their literacy and numeracy potential.

This pack assumes some experience in teaching reading. Its aim is to improve understanding of the complex theory and issues concerning dyslexia.

Teachers must pay more than cursory attention to the teaching of written language skills. The effective teaching of reading (OHP 5) requires:

- a knowledge of the basic processes involved;
- the use of a model of reading which allows for teaching methods to be justified;
- the use of a model of reading which gives direction for planning effective treatment programmes.

In this pack attention is directed at the quality of teaching written language skills. Training, however, is of little use unless its application is encouraged. Teachers' efforts will continue to be diminished by the deteriorating quality and appropriateness of the educational environment, by dilapidated school buildings, and the failure of schools to develop whole-school policies where the needs of all pupils are capable of being met.

The order in which sections are presented is one in which a staff-development session could be run. However, readers must feel free to use the material in any order which is appropriate to their needs, leaving sections out if necessary. The OHPs in each section can be photocopied and used as handouts.

Successful staff development depends very largely on your ability to respond to the immediate feedback from the participants. From this array of OHPs you can select as you go in order to attain the objectives of your in-service training. There are overheads which are more suited to an audience of nursery and primary teachers, others may be suited to in-service for parents. The OHPs are intended as 'pegs' on which to hang your delivery. The structure of your delivery can be determined by the set of OHPs you decide to use. Perhaps the most difficult lesson to learn, when faced with a surfeit of material, is to resist the temptation to rush from one OHP to another without giving time for some of the participants to absorb that which they require. Treat your audience like the class you teach infrequently. Aim your material to suit the majority and hope that the opportunities given for questions will help those who require additional information. Generally, in an adult audience, the range of knowledge is considerable. It is more efficacious to underestimate this knowledge than to overestimate it.

The better you know your topic, the more you are able to respond to the unexpected. The list of recommended books has been carefully assembled to provide a concise but very adequate supply of background material.

Use the OHPs as a basic collection. Add to them whenever you can. Replace those you believe inadequate, outdated, unsuitable with ones of your own choice. Not all that is newly published is more valuable than older material.

Errata

Please note the corrections to page 7 of *Dyslexia: A Staff Development Handbook*.

Ways of Using the Pack

1) A Non-Contact Day

Opening Session: 'Looking at reading'

The group examines the nature of reading and the controversy over falling standards, examines the types of reading they set pupils and the assumptions made about the skills their pupils need to utilize this material in their learning (use material from the following chapters: *What is Reading?* [page 8]; *What is Dyslexia?* [page 9]; *Learning to Read* [page 10]; *Standards of Literacy* [page 11]; *Reading and the Brain* [page 13]; *Individual Differences in Reading* [page 15]).

Second Session: 'Dyslexia'

The group examines the issue of dyslexia, arriving at a greater understanding of this area of special educational needs (use *What is Dyslexia?* [page 9]; *Types of Dyslexia* [page 18]; *Developmental Dyslexia – Possible Causes and Effects* [page 21]; *The Incidence of Dyslexia* [page 27]).

Third Session: 'What can be done?'

The group, having previously identified pupils who are thought to have dyslexia, looks at the processes used to arrive at this decision and compares them to those described in *Assessment and Dyslexia* [page 28]. They then consider ways in which they have dealt with the problem and compare those with the ideas contained in *Supporting and Teaching Skills to Pupils with Dyslexia* [page 31].

2) Staff Meeting to Discuss Policy

Photocopy *Assessment and Dyslexia* [page 28] and distribute to staff beforehand. Use this as a basis to open a discussion on the procedures the school should adopt to identify dyslexia, matching it to the procedures and policy for special educational needs in existence.

3) Twilight Session

Photocopy *From Lap Learning to Literacy* [OHP 4] and distribute this to group members who are then asked to indicate to what extent they feel the order is 'correct' and what aspects they feel are missing or should be deleted. This can be followed by a discussion on the importance of involving parents in helping the child with dyslexia and ways this can be linked to ideas in *Supporting and Teaching Skills to Pupils with Dyslexia* [page 31].

The above are three ways in which this booklet can be and has been used. The success of your staff development will rest upon the degree to which you are conversant with the material.

Ways of Using the Pack

1) A Non-Contact Day

Opening Session : 'Looking at reading'

The group examines the nature of reading and the controversy over falling standards, examines the types of reading they set pupils and the assumptions made about the skills their pupils need to utilize this material in their learning (use material from chapters 3, 5, 6, 7 and 8).

Second Session: 'Dyslexia'

The group examines the issue of dyslexia, arriving at a greater understanding of this area of special educational needs (use chapters 4, 9, 10, 11).

Third Session: 'What can be done?'

The group, having previously identified pupils who are thought to have dyslexia, looks at the processes used to arrive at this decision and compares them to those described in chapter 12. They then consider ways in which they have dealt with the problem and compare those with the ideas contained in chapter 13.

2) Staff Meeting To Discuss Policy

Photocopy chapter 12 and distribute to staff beforehand. Use this as a basis to open a discussion on the procedures the school should adopt to identify dyslexia, matching it to the procedures and policy for special educational needs in existence.

3) Twilight Session

Photocopy 'From Lap Learning to Literacy' (OHP 4) and distribute this to group members who are then asked to indicate to what extent they feel the order is 'correct' and what aspects they feel are missing or should be deleted. This can be followed by a discussion on the importance of involving parents in helping the child with dyslexia and ways this can be linked to the ideas in chapter 13.

The above are but three ways in which this booklet can be and has been used. The success of your staff development will rest upon the degree to which you are conversant with the material.

What is Reading?

The reading process

'Reading whether it is defined as literacy, language, arts, English, dyslexia, or backwardness - is the subject of concerned discussion and divisive debate in communities and their legislative bodies, in business and in industry, in academic institutions and professional organisations, as well as among theorists and practitioners.'

Melnick and Merritt (1972)

That discussion and divisive debate continues unabated is hardly surprising, for the reading processes are among the most complex cerebral activities of human functioning. To analyse completely what happens when we read would be the acme of a psychologist's achievement. 'We may not understand reading until we understand thought itself' (Neisser, 1967).

Reading is the self-rewarding cultural activity of participating in the retrieval of thought and language encoded in alphabetical symbols by the automatized scanning of print for the purpose of finding its meaning. It involves the abilities to:

- **Decode** - this involves the ability to analyse features of letters and to ascribe to them their phonemic equivalents and to recognize spelling patterns. When mastered to the level of automaticity, the reader is able to anticipate and accurately guess a word's identity based upon the rapid perception of syllable, letter group, or general word configuration.
- **Lexical Access** - this is the ability to gain access to the word storage centre within the brain and the associated language centres or to effect access through repeated exposure, as with some reflex actions, or when lexical or grammatical cues enable access. Interconnected words, a phrase or sentence permit accurate guessing of new or unfamiliar words. Such contextual information is also used to extract syntactic and semantic relationships between words, and to organize and relate that information to pre-existing knowledge.
- **Organize Text** - this involves the use of intra-word relationships to extract meaning from phrases, sentences and paragraphs. Highly developed text organizational skills encourage chunking of texts to aid in speed and accuracy of comprehension.

Reading has many forms

Reading a novel silently for pleasure would require something different to reading the same text aloud. Difficult material would probably be processed differently from easy material. The quality of text and the way in which it is presented would pose different problems. When quality is poor, guessing may be required to reconstruct the text. Further, it would be necessary to add a subroutine to evaluate the task-demands in any reading situation and select the most appropriate strategy.

What is Dyslexia?

The word dyslexia is derived from Greek: *dys* (poor or inadequate); and *lexis* (words). The English meaning is *poor or inadequate language.* Dyslexia is characterised by problems in expressive or receptive, oral or written language. Problems may emerge in reading, spelling, writing, speaking or listening.

Dyslexia is not a disease; it has no cure. Dyslexia describes a different kind of mind - often gifted and productive - that learns differently. Intelligence is not the problem. Dyslexic people may have average to superior intelligence. An unexpected gap exists between their learning aptitude and their achievement in school.

The problem is not behavioural. It is not psychological. It is not social. It is not a problem of vision; dyslexic people do not 'see backward'. Dyslexia results from differences in the structure and function of the brain.

Each dyslexic has individual strengths and weaknesses. Many dyslexics are creative and have unusual talent in areas such as art, athletics, architecture, graphics, electronics, mechanics, drama, music or engineering. Dyslexics often show special talent in areas that require visual, spatial, and motor integration.

Their problems in language processing distinguish them as a group. This means that the dyslexic has problems translating language to thought (as in listening or reading) or in translating thought to language (as in writing or speaking).

Characteristics that may accompany dyslexia

1. Lack of awareness of sound in words - sound order, rhymes, or sequence of syllables.
2. Difficulty decoding words - single word identification.
3. Poor sequencing of numbers, of letters in words, when read or written, e.g. b-d, sing-sign, left-felt, 12-21.
4. Difficulty in expressing thought in written form.
5. A history of delayed speech and language development.
6. Imprecise or incomplete interpretation of language that is heard.
7. Difficulty pronouncing multi-syllabic words.
8. Bizarre spelling.
9. Confusion about directions in space or time (right and left, up and down, early and late, yesterday and tomorrow, months and days).
10. Confusion about right- or left- handedness.
11. Difficulty in handwriting.
12. Use of mirror writing.
13. Difficulty in mathematics - often related to sequencing of steps or directionality, or to the language of mathematics.
14. Difficulty learning tables.
15. Poor visual memory.
16. Poor auditory short-term/working memory.
17. Early clumsiness.
18. Easily distracted.
19. Similar problems among relatives.

Learning to Read

The emergence of literacy

Children acquire a great deal of knowledge about spoken language before they show an interest in reading. Although printed language is not speech in print, for printed language is much more precise, formal and complete than everyday speech, there is little doubt that proficiency in this aspect of language is extremely helpful in the acquisition of written language skills.

The ability to comprehend spoken language is the most important factor in learning to read. Although the early years are critical, the acquisition of spoken language does not end before learning to read begins and the overlap is greater than it was thought to be. Fundamental changes continue to take place in children's language beyond the age of five years. To be fully competent, the language user has to broaden lexical and syntactic competence and such linguistic skills continue to develop well into adolescence.

The knowledge children have of grammar, which gives them the competence to produce and comprehend many types of sentence used by the language community in which they live, is not self-taught. It requires a special kind of fit between adult behaviour and infant behaviour. That fit is pre-adapted: it comes to each child as a birthright, both as a result of biological propensities and as a result of social processes of learning transmitted by each new generation.

Parents facilitate the emergence of both oral language and literacy but seldom do it through direct instruction - rather, however, by a system akin to osmosis. The children's experience of both oral language and literacy is holistic, embedded in other objectives which parents have for their children (OHPs 1, 2, 3, 4).

Emerging problems

For children who are not favoured by a healthy parental language acquisition support system (LASS), help is required to ensure their language acquisition device (LAD) receives adequate stimulation. Similarly, those with little experience of being read to, may have little knowledge of what reading is, of its purpose and of the relationship between reading and writing.

However, the majority of preschool children have reading abilities which they fail or are not encouraged to manifest in the early stages of formal reading instruction.

For example:
- when children from different cultural backgrounds who could not write were encouraged to pretend to do so (scribble) there was a recognizable likeness to their national scripts;
- many four-year-old children are able to name letters, spell three-letter words and match common words with pictures;
- if print is decontextualised, as it frequently is in the early stages of formal reading instruction, it can be a source of problems.

Teachers should evaluate literacy achievements of children when they enter school in order to match the needs of each child with suitable early reading activities. There should be no implicit assumption that all children need to proceed from the same point and to have to go through the same activities.

Standards of Literacy

Continuing Concerns

The Bullock Report (1975) pointed out that in respect of the ability to read with understanding and insight, 'as many as one third of the population may be incompetent'. The Adult Literacy and Basic Skills Unit (ALBSU) suggests this may be as high as 13 per cent. In England, six adults in every hundred (about two million people) are said to be 'functionally illiterate', that is, are unable to cope effectively with everyday reading skills. It is against this background that we need to look at what is going on in our schools.

Have things changed since Dr Vera Southgate (Southgate et al, 1981) investigated what teachers were doing to extend the reading abilities of seven to eight year-olds? She found that the children were getting no more than an average of 30 seconds individual help at a time. What they needed at this important stage in their education, she considered, were longer periods of individual help for, say, 15 to 20 minutes.

Have things changed since the Maxwell (1977) study found that functional literacy was not taught, that inadequate attention was given to matching pupils' reading abilities to their text books across the curriculum in secondary schools, and that 'over half the good readers and three quarters of the poor readers failed to make any progress in their reading status from the age of 12 years onwards'?

When Turner (1988) set the reading standards hare coursing again, it was not a fall of standards that should have been our concern - for that is something extremely difficult if not impossible to measure without a great deal more reliable information than is available at present. Nor should the concern about methods of teaching reading claim our attention, for the NFER report commissioned by CATE (Pumfrey and Reason, 1991) belies any fears we might have concerning heavy bias in student preparation in favour of one particular method of teaching reading.

It is difficult to refute the fact that despite masses of research (20,000 papers published between 1964 and 1970 on dyslexia alone) and a considerable implosion of resources (both personnel and material) we do not appear to have made great inroads into the numbers of children who leave school without realizing their reading potential.

This undoubted failure fuels the debate about the teaching of literacy skills. As Moss (1996) comments, the debate is more often informed by dogma than empirical evidence.

'The controversy has a political perspective. When evidence such as the recent Ofsted survey of reading standards in three London boroughs reveals that 20 per cent of seven year olds failed to score when tested, there is a clamour for something to be done about it! Politicians seize upon so-called "falling literacy standards" to question the efficacy of different methods of teaching, and to call for a return to "traditional" teaching approaches.

The debate about the teaching of literacy skills is more often informed by dogma than empirical evidence. Chris Woodhead, the Chief Inspector of Schools, states reasonably enough that the foundations of literacy must be securely established at the primary stage. But he also blames what he believes are the prevailing ideologies of child-centered teaching and discovery learning that militate against children learning the basic skills of reading and writing. DfEE reports have stated that "teachers do not have a conceptual map of reading development" (DfEE, 1993).

But is this really an accurate picture of most teachers' beliefs and practices? What is the evidence for these assumptions? In a recent study of the approaches to literacy taken by primary and secondary teachers, researchers at the University of Bristol discovered that teachers do not hold fixed and rigid views based on any one teaching method. Teachers generally recognize that the teaching and learning of literacy skills is a complex process requiring a range of approaches (Webster et al, 1996). Their problem is more one of developing a strategy for literacy development within the prevailing organisational demands.'

Moss (1996)

Reading and the Brain

The Brain

Our very early development is of crucial importance to us. From the time when our brain was no more than a single neural plate of some 125,000 cells to its full development of some one hundred billion neurons we are dependent on and influenced by our environment.

Alter the environment and another aspect of the vast genetic potential will be activated. Probably no more than 10 per cent of the genes in the mammalian cell are activated in an individual's lifetime.

We have a fairly detailed knowledge of the main areas of the brain involved in speech, in the understanding of spoken language, in reading and in writing.

The idea that a single area of the brain can be related to a single behavioural ability (cerebral localization) has been hotly contested. However, there is enough evidence to support the belief that there are primary areas, but that these have to be seen in the context of the brain as a whole.

The areas said to be associated with speaking, listening, reading, writing and signing are located around the Rolando and Sylvian fissures. The Wernicke's area is concerned with the comprehension of speech, and the Broca's area in the encoding of speech. The Heschl's area concerns auditory reception and the Exner's centre is thought to control writing.

We know that in the majority of people, speech and language primary areas are in the left hemisphere of the brain (OHPs 7, 8).

Reading Processes

The left hemisphere

The process of reading aloud involves, firstly, the Visual Cortex (5) which in turn activates the Wernicke's Area (4) via the angular gyrus. At this point it is thought to be joined by associated auditory representations from the Auditory Cortex (3). The stimulation in the Wernicke's Area is transmitted to the Broca's Area (1) for encoding. The coded programmes are then passed on to the adjacent Motor Area (2) which governs the articulatory response (OHP 13).

Some support for the localization theory comes from studies which found that damage to certain areas of the brain correlated with loss of certain kinds of ability.

However, now that there is a greater array of neurodiagnostic procedures available, there is evidence which runs counter to a simplistic localization theory - for example, studies which measure cerebral or cortical blood-flow show a far more complex involvement of different parts of the brain although broadly speaking the primary areas remain.

The right hemisphere

The most general statement that can be made about right-hemisphere specializations is that they are non-linguistic functions that seem to involve complex visual and spatial processes.

A comparatively new way to conceptualize hemispheric difference is, instead of a breakdown based on the type of tasks (for example, verbal and spatial) best performed by each hemisphere, a dichotomy based on different ways of dealing with information in general.

According to this analysis, the left hemisphere is specialized for language functions, but these specializations are as a consequence of the left hemisphere's superior analytical skills, of which language is one manifestation. Similarly, the right hemisphere's superior visuospatial performance derives from its synthetic, holistic manner of dealing with information.

It also suggested that the two hemispheres differ in the kinds of information they pick up from visual stimuli.

Because both spatial orientation and shape discrimination are typically linked to right-hemisphere functions, it could be argued that the initial stages of learning to read are linked with the right hemisphere. When perceptual analysis of the features of text become automatized, as in the competent reader's performance, the reader's focus is on semantic and syntactic analyses. These processes are, in the main, controlled by the left hemisphere (Pumfrey and Reason, 1991).

Some pupils fail to make progress in learning to read because they do not make the hemispheric shift (Bakker, 1990).

Effective reading requires the involvement of both hemispheres

Almost any human behaviour or higher mental function, however, clearly involves more than the actual specialities of either hemisphere and utilizes what is common to both. OHP 12 illustrates both hemispheres' involvement in a reading process.

'In research with split-brain subjects, languages continue to stand out as the most salient and profound difference between left brain and right brain. Some investigators have claimed that all other hemisphere differences are manifestations of the verbal asymmetry. They argue that the region of the left hemisphere that developed spatialization for language would no longer be available to handle the processing of spatial information formally controlled by either half of the brain. The right hemisphere, then, would appear specialized for spatial skills, although its specialization was really a result of the left hemisphere's deficit rather than the right hemisphere's superiority. This argument provides an interesting perspective to the problem of how lateralization developed ...'

Springer and Deutch (1989)

Models of the brain

In order to conceptualize our limited understanding of the brain, we have tried to make models to explain it coherently. One such model suggests the brain has three functional units which are involved in all cerebral activity:

- the regulation of our level of arousal or wakefulness;
- obtaining, processing and storing information from our senses;
- programming, regulating and verifying our mental activity.

However, the cognitive sciences only provide partial knowledge of the brain and its processes. We are still only at the frontiers of understanding the chemistry of the neuron. We know much about the attributes of the memory but do not know how memories are laid down, stored and retrieved. We know that adverse genetic and environmental factors can so easily upset the learning processes, yet we also know of the plasticity of the brain, particularly the young brain, which can learn to perform functions after the areas deemed to control them have apparently been completely destroyed.

We should not be either surprised or disappointed, therefore, if we still cannot fully explain why and how we learn to read and why some children appear to acquire literacy skills as if through a process of osmosis and others appear to struggle and require support throughout their lives.

Individual Differences in Reading

To observe differences between poor and good readers is a common research practice. When differences are found the question that invariably follows is: Do the differences tell us about the causes of reading difficulties or are they the consequences of them? Unfortunately, correlations are not necessarily indicators of causal relationships. Furthermore, a correlation alone does not show in which direction it runs so we are often left with assumptions about which comes first - differences as causes or differences as consequences.

If individual differences in reading are on a continuum of reading ability then the same forces affect good and poor readers alike. What is good for one is good for all. If, however, the factors associated with individual differences in reading are peculiar to them then it is necessary to differentiate teaching systems, methods and materials. Different difficulties usually require different remedies (OHP 17).

For the majority of adults the memories of learning to read can be recalled no more clearly than learning to talk or walk. For most people learning to read was a smooth process uninterrupted by the transition from home to school tuition. Written language skills appear to be acquired more or less adequately irrespective of whether a meaning-emphasis or code-emphasis approach was used or whether traditional orthography, (t.o.), or the initial teaching alphabet (i.t.a.) was used.

The poor reader

Many poor readers produce comparatively low scores in verbal intelligence tests in comparison to their performance on non-verbal intelligence tests. Pupils comprehend text only in relation to what they know. In this sense, therefore, reading differences are a matter of differences in knowledge.

There is evidence that the reliance on phonics decreases with age in proficient readers but not in poor readers. Poor readers in comparison to good readers use fewer semantic, syntactic and text-meaning cues.

Poor readers are more limited in their use of reading strategies and generally field-dependent. For example, good readers are more accurate at predicting print - guessing what comes next - than poor readers. Good readers self-correct responses which violate contextual information more efficiently than poor readers. Perhaps their reading is more automatized and allows time for monitoring their own efforts. The expert in many skills appears to have far more time than the less skilled to choose appropriate responses (OHPs 18, 19).

Good readers are faster as well as more accurate in decoding than poor readers. Decoding latency is less for high-frequency words than it is for low-frequency words, less for shorter words than longer words and greater as the syllables within words increase. Modified texts such as hand-outs for children with learning difficulties do not always take cognizance of such facts.

As reading proficiency increases a greater use is made of 'analogy' - that is when a new string of letters is pronounced by not referring to general rules but by comparing the current word with words of known pronunciation (OHP 20). Poor readers are unlikely to develop this skill.

The person with dyslexia

The degree of difficulty a person with dyslexia has with written language and/or speaking varies from person to person due to inherited differences in the brain, in its development as well as the type of teaching the person receives.

The strengths and weaknesses in brain functioning displayed by those with dyslexia are no different from those in the general population with the exception that the strengths are less likely to emanate from the language areas. To call dyslexia a learning difficulty tends to infer that the dyslexic cannot learn. But with the proper instruction, pupils with dyslexia do learn. A better appreciation of the special needs of these pupils may result from using the term *learning difference* rather than *learning disability*.

Each individual with dyslexia is unique, but the vast majority will respond positively to a well-designed multi-sensory approach. Such individuals become doctors, barristers, engineers, architects, artists and teachers. They probably do not become speedy shorthand or court typists. *The expertise of the teacher is the key*. The more severe the learning differences, the greater the need for an individualized, multi-sensory, sequential approach.

The underachieving person

The measurement of under-functioning, that is the degree to which a reading score predicted from an intelligence quotient is higher than the achieved reading score is sometimes used to support a diagnosis of dyslexia but also, and perhaps more importantly, to determine whether or not a child warrants statementing for special educational needs.

Similar caution is necessary in using measurements of under-functioning for predictive purposes as is taken with the use of intelligence quotients.

The correlations between IQs and reading quotients vary considerably depending, in part, upon the tests used.

Predictions of reading abilities from IQs and vice versa are, at best, 'guesstimates'. In helping to direct intervention it is far better to base short-term predictions upon calculations which estimate zones of proximal development that children may have in the various domains.

There is a vast disparity between the majority and the disadvantaged minority of children in their level of performance in intelligence or achievement tests. We need to accept the existence of inequalities however they have come about (i.e. social disadvantage, constitutional difficulties, poor health etc.) and the gap in cognitive competence between the 'haves' and 'have nots' without being bothered by the question 'which causes which?' and concentrate upon being able to reduce or remove the temporary retardation detected by standardized intelligence or achievement tests.

Rather than restricting testing to a child's present ability to respond to information already acquired, learning assessment potential embeds training in a test-train-test sequence. The student first views and attempts solution of the reasoning problem in a traditional format. Subsequently the child is shown how the problems may be solved and is offered a problem-related training. Following the training, the child is reassessed. The intention of learning-potential assessment is to obtain an estimate of general ability derived from reasoning problems of suitable difficulty which the child has an opportunity to learn how to solve, and which permit a comparison with the low scholastic aptitude score. If a child can demonstrate, following a short period of training, that he/she can perform at a level approximating average peer performance we can assume that he/she has the ability to profit from experience (which reflects some educationalists' definition of intelligence).

Vygotsky describes the zone of proximal development as the distance between the level of performance a child can reach unaided and the level of participation that can be accomplished when guided by a more knowledgeable participant. For some children in a particular domain this zone may be particularly small, the interpretation being that the child is not yet ready to participate at a more mature level than his/her unaided performance would indicate. For another child in that domain or that child in another domain, the zone of proximal development can be quite large, indicating that with aid, the child can participate much more fully and maturely in the activity than one might suppose on the basis of only unaided performance.

The amount of improvement a child makes in a test-train-test project in a determined domain will indicate the zone of proximal development that a child may have in that domain much more accurately than a measured IQ or some 'guesstimate' of performance in another domain derived from that IQ.

Types of Dyslexia (OHP 21)

Acquired dyslexia

Readers who, after brain injury, can no longer read, are said to have acquired dyslexia. The common strand within children and young people who have acquired dyslexia is that they have damage to the brain which affects their ability to process written language. The efficiency of the reading process can be interrupted by damage to numerous parts of the brain.

Damage to areas identified as being responsible for written language skills, typically components of the left hemisphere, may produce specific types of reading and writing deficits. Brain injury to parts of the brain during the developmental period in children may produce specific impairments in written language abilities.

Although 'acquired dyslexia' is thought of as a distinct group, those concerned are far from being homogeneous. Injuries to different parts of the brain result in very different behaviours in written language skills, but within the diversities there are sufficient patterns which have encouraged descriptions of forms or syndromes of acquired dyslexia, described below.

Deep dyslexia

Deep dyslexia involves two malfunctions:

- a severe impairment to, or even a loss of, the ability to convert graphemes to phonemes without lexical involvement; and
- lack of connections between entries in the visual input-lexicon which contains specifications for recognizing words and their corresponding phonological entries in an output-lexicon for speech production.

Reading for deep dyslexics relies heavily on access from a graphic representation of a written letter-string to an entry in the input-lexicon, then to a semantic representation of that word's meaning, and thence to an entry in the output-lexicon which will meet the semantic specification.

Shallice and Warrington (1980) suggest the syndrome can be defined by four key features:

1. The deep dyslexic has a very great difficulty in using the phonological route in reading. Their performance in reading nonsense words is extremely poor.
2. Word reading performance is influenced by parts of speech, in order: nouns (best), adjectives, verbs, function words (worst).
3. There is a large effect of imageability/concreteness on word reading performance.
4. Errors of visual (team/tease), semantic (clown/circus), and derivational (think/ thinking) types are made.

Coltheart (1984) argues that deep dyslexics may not be able to use the left hemisphere at all. They rely on right-hemisphere processing to aid global and pictorial recognition in conjunction with semantic and contextual clues.

A list of symptoms which constitutes the symptom complex of deep dyslexia is as follows:

1. Semantic errors (act - play, dinner - food).
2. Visual errors (stock - shock, quiz - queue).
3. Function-word substitution (for - and, the - yes).

18

4. Derivational errors (wise - wisdom, birth - born).
5. Non-lexical derivation of phonology from print is impossible (reading non-words aloud).
6. Lexical derivation from print is impaired (errors in whole-word retrieval).
7. Low imageability words harder to read aloud than high imageability words.
8. Verbs harder to read aloud than adjectives which are harder than nouns.
9. Function words are harder to read aloud than content words.
10. Writing, spontaneously, or to dictation, is impaired.
11. Auditory-verbal short-term memory is impaired.
12. Whether a word can be read aloud at all depends on its context.

Phonological dyslexia

Phonological core deficits entail difficulty making use of phonological information when processing written and oral language. The major components of phonological deficits involve phonemic awareness, sound-symbol relations, and storage and retrieval of phonological information in memory. Problems with phonemic awareness are most prevalent and can coexist with difficulties in storage and retrieval among children with dyslexia who have phonological deficits.

Phonemic awareness refers to one's understanding of and access to the sound structure of language. For example, children with dyslexia have difficulty segmenting words into individual syllables or phonemes and have trouble blending speech sounds into words.

Storage of phonological information during reading involves creating a sound-based representation of written words in working memory. Deficits in the storage of phonological information result in faulty representations in memory that lead to inaccurate applications of sound rules during reading tasks.

Retrieval of phonological information from long-term memory refers to how the child remembers pronunciations of letters, word segments, or entire words.

Phonological dyslexia is a form of reading disorder in which the ability to read unfamiliar words, or pronounceable non-words, is selectively deficient. It occurs both as a developmental dyslexia (i.e. a specific pattern of reading difficulty seen in some children as they are learning to read) and as an acquired dyslexia (i.e. a specific pattern of reading impairment in people who were normal readers but who then suffered brain damage which affected their reading). The disorder therefore has implications for our understanding both of how children learn to read and the architecture of the reading system used for normal skilled reading.

Surface dyslexia

There are two impairments minimally necessary to account for the reading of surface dyslexics:

- an impairment of access to the input lexicon from the graphic input; and
- partial impairment or distortion of grapheme-phoneme conversion.

Semantic errors never occur, and if the dyslexics show comprehension it is almost always of the error rather than the target (listen-liston-boxer).

The surface dyslexic finds it difficult to read irregular words. Quite often they read these words phonologically and turn them into nonsense words in doing so. They might for example read 'broad' as 'brode'. Another difficulty is that they muddle the meaning of homophones like 'soar' and 'saw'. The surface dyslexic finds it difficult to remember what words look like, and they depend too heavily on working out their meaning through rules about letter sound relationships (Bradley & Bryant, 1985).

For those who have surface dyslexia the problems appear to be determined, at least in large part, by the spelling-to-sound characteristics of the word.

Among their problems are:

- a lack of lexical access for words which are read incorrectly and misunderstood;
- a failure in grouping letter strings into appropriate graphemes;
- misapplication or failure to apply certain grapheme-phoneme rules.

It was the striking similarity between acquired dyslexics and the attempts to read by beginners and the errors made by children who find the acquisition of written language skills difficult that many researchers claim support for the concept of specific developmental dyslexia, commonly referred to as dyslexia and now even more frequently as specific learning difficulties (SpLD).

Hyperlexia

Hyperlexia is sometimes referred to as direct dyslexia and is an ability to read material with apparent ease and often well beyond their vocabulary usage but without comprehension. It appears that they are capable of converting print to speech using phonological skills and whole-word recognition strategies. Their problem seems to be that they can make no sense of the text.

Developmental dyslexia

Although there is some debate about the subtyping of acquired dyslexia, for the most part there is agreement that as a whole it relates very largely to people who have lost some of their capacity for written language skills following brain injury.

People with developmental dyslexia rarely have the hard neurological signs typical of people with acquired dyslexia. Definitions are rarely clear cut. Exclusions, identification by negative criteria, are used to distinguish those with developmental dyslexia from other poor readers. For example, the definition provided by the World Federation of Neurology (Critchley, 1970) refers to developmental dyslexia as '... a disorder manifested by difficulty in learning to read despite conventional instruction, adequate intelligence and sociocultural opportunity'.

'Specific Developmental Dyslexia refers more particularly (than dyslexia) to difficulties in learning to read occurring essentially in the absence of significantly low ability, serious illness, emotional disturbance, cultural or material deprivation, or shortcomings in the educational process itself. Some or other of these factors may be found in association, as aggravating causes, but are not primary in causal significance.'

Pumfrey and Reason (1991)

It is the condition of developmental dyslexia which is commonly referred to as dyslexia, and it is so used in the rest of this text.

Developmental Dyslexia - Possible Causes and Effects

These terms are used to describe the condition of those pupils whose extreme difficulties in learning to read cannot be accounted for by lack of ability or opportunity.

Dominance and laterality

The functional relationship between the brain's two hemispheres has been a major focus for research. Each hemisphere has its own role, being more involved in the performance of some activities and less in others. A hemisphere is said to be dominant if it plays the leading part in an aspect of mental functioning (OHPs 8, 9, 10).

Lateralization is the development of these functions in the different hemispheres. Briefly, the left hemisphere is superior in the use of language, and in those analyses involving temporal discriminations, whereas the right hemisphere is superior in the analysis of parallel events such as body orientation and the recognition of form and spatial relationships. The left hemisphere is dominant for the vast majority of right-handed people and, perhaps surprisingly, for many left-handed people.

The two walnut-like halves of a person's brain are not of equal size. The left hemisphere is for the majority of us not only larger, but its surface, the cerebral cortex, is more deeply fissured and convoluted.

Poor development of the left hemisphere and over development on the right could, it is thought by Masland (1990), result in an imbalance in the interaction of the two hemispheres and may account for the confusion observed by Orton (1925) in children with written language problems who exhibit mirror writing or letter reversals. Orton postulated that the dyslexic individual suffered from confusion of left and right information, with a tendency to use mirror image information coming from the right side rather than the correct image from the same side as the language centre.

There are people who have hemispheres that do not show clear cut dominance for certain activities. Some display a cross laterality that is usually interpreted as having a dominant eye on the opposite side to the dominant hand. There are others who display a pattern of mixed dominance throughout the body e.g. right-handed, left-footed and right-eyed.

The specialized functions of the hemispheres and their neurophysiological bases are, as yet, only partly understood.

Some tests of dyslexia which collect data concerning established eye or hand preference and evidence of cross or mixed laterality imply that it has some significance in the acquisition of written language skills. Several major research studies, for example Clark (1970), Isle of Wight Study/Rutter, Tizard and Whitmore (1970) and The National Child Development Study/Whittington and Richards (1987), failed to find any laterality measures which were significant in distinguishing between children with specific reading problems.

Cerebral dominance

The superiority of one side of the brain for a particular function is called cerebral dominance.

Each half of the brain is dominant for several functions. For example, the left side is usually dominant for language, and the right side for spatial abilities. Asymmetry of development is found in the human foetus at thirty-one weeks of intra-uterine life suggesting that dominance is genetically determined.

Dominance has usually been regarded as a unique biological feature of humans but it is now known that it is present in other species. Bird song, for example, is much more seriously affected by damage to one side of their brain.

Laterality

Laterality is the preference for using the right or left side of the body. Lateralization of language function in the dominant hemisphere occurs at an earlier age in girls than in boys.

Left-handers have less anatomical asymmetry than right handers, a finding concordant with other data showing that functional dominance is less marked in left-handers. Thus left-handers more often have the ability to be mixed-dominant.

Language and handedness have long been two major factors in any discussion of cerebral dominance. The left hemisphere is dominant for language in most right-handed people, whereas 60 per cent of left-handers are either dominant and/or greatly involve the left hemisphere. The pattern of mixed dominance throughout the body, a not uncommon finding, has further complicated investigations.

Cross-laterality, such as a preference for the use of the left hand accompanied by a preference for the right eye for sighting, has been regarded by some researchers as a contributory factor to children's learning difficulties and to reading difficulties in particular.

Localization

The theory that a certain area of the brain can be related to certain behavioural ability, such as vision or speech, is known as cerebral localization.

There is an alternative theory of equipotentiality - that is that every region of the brain is equally involved in all activities. However, there is increasing evidence that there may be primary areas with other areas making a contribution.

More recently in the literature there is increasing attention paid to the interconnections between the specialized function of the two hemispheres of the brain.

Farnham-Diggory (1978) further suggests that learning disabilities may occur in three different areas:

- there may be a problem in moving information from one hemisphere to another;
- there may be a task-specific problem with one of the hemispheres so that it performs inadequately when it takes its turn;
- there may be a task-specific problem of overall control.

At the same time Farnham-Diggory suggests that we know only five things for sure:

1. It is possible for one hemisphere to take control of a simple task that is presented - through the ears, eyes or hands - to both hemispheres at once.
2. These dominance effects may change with development.
3. The effects may not be the same for males and females.
4. They may not be the same for dyslexic and normal children.
5. They may shift as a function of learning sets induced by certain forms of school intervention.

Tansley and Pankhurst (1981) summarized the mass of evidence - much of it conflicting - by saying that the great majority of children with laterality problems have no reading problems and concluded that whilst measures of cerebral dominance and laterality may be of limited value, they may be of more use in combination with other measures.

Visual skills

Reading an English script requires the eye to track from left to right and move from the top line downwards. This requires teaching, for not all written languages follow this pattern. Those who have little experience of 'lap-learning', of seeing finger tracking whilst being read to, are particularly at risk of learning the wrong tracking habit.

For some children with incorrect tracking, reading was made easier by turning the page upside down so that the print could be scanned from right to left. To become a skilled reader of upside down print is hardly satisfactory. Far better to correct the errant behaviour.

The paired-reading system appears to have been shown to be successful with this problem - presumably, because it ensures practising left to right tracking rapidly.

Some children's reading problems may be associated with vision defects. It is recommended that children with apparently intransigent reading problems should be examined by an ophthalmologist.

The right eye for those with left-hemisphere language dominance, is thought to have an important role in learning to read, at the stage when progress is made from reading single words to more fluent reading. This stage is particularly dependent on the use of linguistic content. Competent readers have an asymmetrical visual scan, taking in about 14 characters to the right and about 7 to the left of the fixation point. When children do show symptoms of perceptual problems, working with three-dimensional letters with both eyes covered, has been shown to be effective.

There is evidence (Pavlidis, 1985) that the reading eye movements of children with dyslexia differ from those of normal readers. For example, saccadic eye movements - those are the patterns of eye movements which are displayed when reading or trying to read - are very different for the skilled and unskilled reader. The unskilled reader, makes more fixations and regressions and often fixates for longer periods. The not uncommon problem of determining cause and effect is present in the interpretation of this experimental data. Are the irregular saccadic eye movements the cause of problems in acquiring reading or are they the outcome of the difficulty? If you cannot read fluently, it is hardly surprising that you would search, scan and fixate, looking desperately for cues to help you to get meaning from print.

Saccadic eye movements and smooth tracking, can be affected by even quite low doses of drugs. Some eye tracking problems in dyslexics mirror those of children receiving some types of medication. It is possible that the areas of the brain affected by these drugs are the same areas impaired in some children and which account for the poor integration and regulation of the fine movements so necessary for efficient tracking (OHP 23).

Scotopic sensitivity

Scotopic sensitivity syndrome is said to consist of four types of visual distortion which may cause children difficulty in acquiring fluency in reading:

- Light sensitivity - the ability to accommodate high contrast and glare.
- Visual resolution - the ability to see print clearly without distortion.
- Span of focus - the ability to perceive groups of words at the same
- time.
- Sustain focus - the ability to do tasks with the eyes in a relaxed state with objects of focus (Pumfrey and Reason, 1991).

In the UK it is claimed by the Irlen Institute that between 50 per cent and 75 per cent of learning disabled people suffer from the syndrome. It claims that its technique which involves wearing coloured lens spectacles can result in successful remediation of reading problems. This motivated parental and medical interest in the syndrome.

The evidence is far from conclusive. Many of the reported studies are said to have had very unsatisfactory experimental designs. A major problem is that without an accurately described test of scotopic sensitivity it is impossible for the results of intervention to be replicated.

Interest in the topic has diminished and many of those whose treatment centred on a concentration on the visual function no longer consider it to be the solution to the problem.

Emotional and behaviour difficulties

The frequently reported feelings of frustration, inadequacy and humiliation of children with written language problems whether they be labelled as children with dyslexia or not is familiar to those who teach them. The parents' frustration at their children's lack of progress and the lack of empathy they receive from professionals when they make their complaints is also well documented. It has been suggested that parental distress does not necessarily relate to the extent of the disability but to the values, aspirations, hopes and knowledge of the parents.

Self-concept and motivation

The causal link between poor self-concept and poor reading is well established although the direction of the relationship has yet to be resolved - in the generality of cases, at least.

It seems essential that in the teaching of all children, but particularly those with special educational needs, intervention should take account of the 'whole' child, looking beyond the psychoneurological explanations to the educational environment, and take into account, for example, the sense the child is making of the situation.

Counselling with the objective of self-esteem enhancement or stress reduction can be undertaken by a sympathetic adult who can create an uncritical atmosphere. This is particularly effective when done by those the child holds in esteem. In our own research we found that parental involvement in their children's education was a potent force and there is little doubt that the majority are or can be schooled to be successful 'teachers'. Many of their teaching skills are self-evident in their children's development when they enter school and this needs to be pointed out to them, for the parents of the special needs children often are themselves lacking in self-esteem. They frequently have feelings of guilt about their children's failings.

Miles, quoted in Pumfrey and Reason (1991), takes the view that the term dyslexia assists parents to make sense of occurrences they know to exist. They know their children have difficulty with reading and spelling - they need explanations which remove the sense of blame. Miles sees this as a cornerstone for counselling children and their parents. We do not disagree that the initial classification of dyslexia can be accompanied with a sense of relief but, unless solutions are found to the apparently intransigent problems of acquiring written language skills, the relief can quickly turn to despondency which is counterproductive. Immediate solutions particularly for the older children are rarely forthcoming and the loss of faith in the professional who builds false hopes can be devastating for both child and parent.

Environmental correlates

An overriding factor for many special needs children in ordinary schools, which is crucial in assisting their motivation and in promoting their healthy self-esteem, is a school ethos which fosters a sensitive whole-school policy to learning difficulties. Teachers are the key in this respect as they are in many aspects of the curriculum during the 15,000 hours they act in loco parentis (Rutter et al, 1979; Mortimore et al, 1988).

There are many environmental factors which affect children's ability to learn. Family crises such as death, divorce, alcoholism, drug addiction and mental illness among others can contribute to failure to acquire adequate written language skills. Perhaps of paramount importance is social class. Social class 5 children are said to have 15 times greater chance of being non-readers as those of social class 1. It is not suggested that these factors are determining factors of dyslexia, but they can muddy the diagnostic procedure and make treatment more problematic. It is well to remember that many good readers face identical environmental problems with apparently no such detrimental effects.

Cognitive aspects

The major stages of development of reading are thought to include:

- the logographic stage where words are recognized holistically;
- the alphabetic stage when letter-sound knowledge occurs which enables grapheme-phoneme correspondence to take place;
- the orthographic stage in which the process of word recognition becomes automatized and associations are formed between grapho-phonics, syntactic and semantic elements.

There are many experts who hold that dyslexia is associated with the alphabetic stage.

Association of early rhyming skill with phonological sensitivity and their interaction as a part of a language acquisition device with a critical developmental period has led to a theory that ability at rhyming is an early predictor of subsequent reading skills (Auditory Categorization Test, Bradley, 1984).

It follows from the above that phonemic awareness is a prerequisite of being literate but not everybody holds this view. Literate adults have been shown to lack phonemic segmentation skills so, although there appears to be evidence to support a correlation, we remain ignorant of its direction. It may be that phonological awareness is achieved as a consequence of being literate in an alphabetical and mainly phonetic script.

The problem, it is thought, might lie in the extent to which phonological ability affects the verbal mediation and rehearsal of visual symbols. Naming difficulties have been implicated as a problem for dyslexic children. Speed and ability to retrieve phonological codes from long-term memory could explain such problems. Auditory memory span has been used as an indicator of the presence of dyslexia, though how the efficient reciting of digits (a digit span test is often a part of a battery of tests of dyslexia) can be used to distinguish between the phonological aspects of memory is not clear.

Memory span (e.g. sentence memory span) and reading comprehension are thought to be correlated. However, if decoding ability is controlled the measures of memory span and of comprehension are inseparable.

Speed of articulation has been linked with memory span. The articulatory time loop through repetition extends the time limit of the short-term phonological store. Auditory memory span for script appears to improve with reading. Dyslexic children have been shown to have more difficulty than reading-age-matched children in tasks requiring nonsense word recognition.

Many language-disordered children are known to have specific difficulty in immediate auditory memory span. The problem lies in a capacity limitation in the phonological short-term store of working memory which restricts the ability to acquire phonological representations through repetition.

Sequencing difficulties are associated with traditionally held concepts of dyslexia. More recently these problems have been ascribed to inadequate learning experience and limited auditory memory span.

Clumsiness is claimed to be associated with dyslexia. Clumsiness, like so many other classifications in educational practice, has a conceptual specificity but is a heterogeneous condition. It is reported that clumsiness caused by motor disorder is associated with speech disordered children - the production of speech is a motor function. It is also associated with more generalized learning difficulties. It appears self-evident that motor difficulties can be related to writing problems and thus contribute to spelling problems but it seems most unlikely that they are primary problems with regard to literacy.

The effects of drugs

Piracetum - This drug has a 20 year history in the treatment of memory problems in the elderly. Its effects on children with dyslexia was to show improvements in a range of performance indicators including reading skills, verbal memory, verbal comprehension and the ability to process letter-like stimuli. What happens in the long term when medication ceased is not recorded.

Antihistamines - The use of antihistamines with dyslexics who have a cerebellar-vestibular disorder which makes them prone to feelings of motion sickness and is associated with problems in processing textual material which appears to move has been claimed to have some measure of therapeutic success.

Anti-Motion Sickness Pills - The possibility exists that the problem which dyslexic children appear to have in acquiring automaticity, that is achieving an automatic performance in a skill, might be improved if the problem of processing textual material is reduced by the administration of anti-motion sickness drugs.

Vitamin Tablets - Vitamins and minerals taken in high doses have been claimed to improve learning ability, and increases in intelligence have been reported. It seems sensible to adjust an unsatisfactory diet with vitamin and mineral supplements but when sufficient vitamins and minerals abound, excess intake of some vitamins can be toxic. The effects of vitamin supplementation in general and on children with dyslexia is far from clear as are speculations about zinc deficiency, insufficiency of essential fatty acids, and lead pollution.

Genetics

As yet, there is no guaranteed marker phenotype that appears early in development, persists, and is specifically linked to dyslexia. There are several good candidates:

1. phoneme awareness and segmentation skills;
2. verbal short-term memory and lexical retrieval.

Glossary

Genotype   -   generally it can refer to the entire genetic constitution of an individual.

Phenotype   -   the observable characteristics of an individual, the result of genetic and environmental influences.

The Incidence of Dyslexia

As there is no universally agreed definition of dyslexia or universally agreed criteria for diagnosis, it is not surprising that there is no figure for the incidence of dyslexia, only a range of figures.

The range extends from less than one per cent in Japan to more than 25 per cent elsewhere. The estimates vary from country to country, area to area, specialist to specialist and from researcher to researcher. There have been many studies which have attempted to determine the incidence of severe reading disability in the general population.

Clark (1970): All the children born in the County of Dumbartonshire in a five-month period were tested after they had completed two years at school and were aged about seven years. 15 per cent (N=1544) of these pupils still had no independent reading skill.

Rutter and Yule (1975): Using regression analysis with reading and ability test scores as variables, Rutter and Yule identified a group of children who had a discrepancy between their observed reading scores and their predicted reading scores of 28 months and labelled them as being specifically reading retarded (3.5 per cent of ten-year-olds were so classified, 4.5 per cent of fourteen-year-olds on the Isle of Wight, and 6 per cent of ten-year-olds in the London area).

Dobbins (1986, 1990): Dobbins tested a population of 5000 fourth year junior pupils in a LEA. Using regression analysis with scores obtained on the Raven's Standard Progressive Matrices and the NFER Reading Test BD as variables, he classified seven groups. Severe underachievers were those whose underachievement could not readily be explained.

Frost and Emery (1995): Approximately 3 to 6 per cent of all school-aged children are believed to have developmental reading disabilities, or dyslexia. In fact, almost 50 per cent of children receiving special education have learning disabilities, and dyslexia is the most prevalent form.

National Institutes of Health publications estimate that as many as 15 per cent of us are dyslexic. Dyslexia occurs among all groups regardless of race, age or income.

Evidence in the U.K. argues for a broad cluster of children with severe difficulties in written language skills of between 1 and 3 per cent of the population.

Assessment and Dyslexia

Many reading authorities refute the assumptions inherent in dyslexia. They argue that children's difficulties in learning to read are very largely because they are less mature or less capable than the majority of children of the same chronological age in the development of the competencies required for a satisfactory acquisition of written language skills. They would argue the identification of dyslexia as psuedo-science.

Pseudo-science it may be but '... there is also the legal position that dyslexia exists and can be identified. If professionals cannot agree, the court will decide whether or not the evidence presented establishes the case for such classification of a pupil' (Chasty & Friel, 1991).

There are many practitioners who, in full knowledge of the evidence for and against the concept of dyslexia, use an identification procedure which selects subsets of poor readers who they categorize as children with dyslexia. The variations of subsets within the populations of poor readers are of course limitless. In addition, the choice of characteristics which are used to identify the subsets leads to the determination of cut-off points which distinguish the mild, the moderate and the severe categories of learning difficulties. This is seen to be necessary in order to decide whether statements of special educational needs are required.

The variations of the criteria used to identify sub-groups of children with written language difficulties who require statementing as pupils with dyslexia are considerable both within and between authorities.

There is a plethora of tests that claim to differentiate between children with dyslexia and other pupils with severe and prolonged reading difficulties.

Informed professional judgement is required concerning which, if any, of such tests are needed to determine what help is necessary for children to learn to become literate and numerate.

The following are examples of tests quoted in reports which support requests for statementing:

The *Bangor Dyslexia Test*, although not intended as a means of definitive diagnosis is, nevertheless, used as supportive evidence. Despite the considerable reputation of its author, the test has been severely criticized on technical grounds. Much further work needs to be done before it can be used with confidence (Pumfrey, 1985).

Psychologists frequently quote the atypical profiles of sub-test scores of such tests as the *Kaufmann-ABC*, the *Weschler Intelligence Scale for Children*, or the *British Abilities Scale*.

The four sub-tests of the twelve sub-tests of the W.I.S.C., considered to have particular relevance in the profiles of dyslexic pupils, are **Arithmetic**, **Coding**, **Information** and **Digit Span** (ACID).

If pupils score low on these sub-tests in comparison to their scores on other sub-tests then this is taken as support for a diagnosis of dyslexia. It is not unusual for the scores on these four sub-tests to be disregarded when calculations of intelligence are being made.

Several systems of determining the severity of the discrepancy between the performance of pupils on the four sub-tests and those on the remaining sub-tests have been advanced. Among them are:

1. The intelligence of the pupils when calculated by pro-rating the eight remaining sub-tests should be at least average or above average whilst those of the four critical sub-tests would be comparatively poor - probably below average intelligence.

   This system restricts support for a classification of children with dyslexia to those of average or above average intelligence. The better the poor readers perform on the intelligence test, particularly if the profile contains an ACID profile, the more certain is the claim for the diagnosis of dyslexia.

2. The ratio between the sum of the four sub-test scores and the sum of the remainder is calculated. When that ratio reaches say 1:4 then the degree of disparity is such as to warrant support for dyslexia.

   This system has the support of some practitioners because it does not rule out children who measure on intelligence tests as below average intelligence. They argue that if dyslexia has causal constitutional disabilities then it would not be restricted to any particular sub-groups determined by measurements of intelligence.

3. A variation of 2 above is the use of the sum of the ACID four to determine a fraction of the total intelligence sub-tests including the four. A somewhat different sub-group of poor readers is said to be identified.

All three of the above selective methods have the disadvantage that the children with relatively even profiles who cannot read are excluded from the diagnosed classification. The children so excluded are plentiful. They are children whose profiles show a marked discrepancy between observed reading age and the predicted age from their performance on an intelligence test. The concept of underfunctioning justifiably has its critics, but providing it is treated with caution it can prove useful in drawing attention to children who can so easily be overlooked because their reading age often matches their chronological age.

Patterns of WISC-R

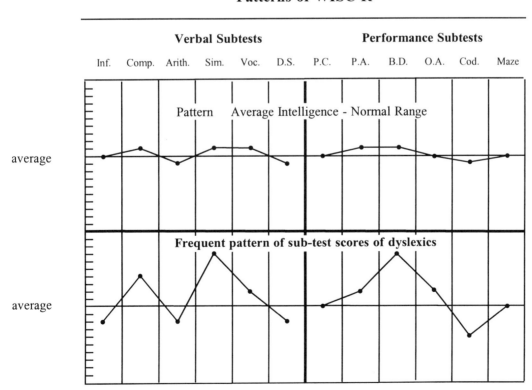

The Dyslexia Early Screening Test (DEST) (4 years 6 months - 6 years 5 months), the Dyslexia Screening Test (DST) (6 years 6 months - 16 years 5 months) and the Dyslexia Adult Screening Test (DAST) have comparatively recently been published. The authors, Dr A. Fawcett and Professor R. Nicholson, write that 'Since the publication of the Bangor test there have been developments in theoretical understanding of the underlying nature of dyslexia which suggests a number of further valuable 'positive indicators' for dyslexia.'

The tests are intended primarily as screening instruments and unlike most psychological tests they have been developed for use by school professionals (teachers, special educational needs co-ordinators or school nurses) - supplied by The Psychological Corporation and published by Harcourt Brace & Company.

A sensitive strategy for identification of dyslexia should ensure (OHP 24):

- that the governors are reminded of their responsibility to use their best endeavours to ensure that the teachers are aware of the importance of identifying and providing for the children in their school who have special educational needs;
- that where a pupil is acknowledged to have special educational needs, those needs are made known to all who are likely to teach him/her;
- the procedure in the school aimed at identifying children likely to have special educational needs is clearly understood;
- that the teachers' implementation of the programme for a child is monitored;
- that there is systematic recording of the assessment of needs and how those needs are to be met;
- that all concerned personnel are fully appraised of the children's needs and how it has been decided those needs should be met (parent, each teacher, each support service including advisers/inspectors, educational psychologists, specialist teachers, education welfare officers, careers officers and staff of health and social services);
- that information is published concerning the provision available in the school to meet children's needs.

Supporting and Teaching Skills to Pupils with Dyslexia

There is much in teaching approaches originally developed for either normal or undifferentiate poor readers from which pupils with dyslexia will benefit.

However, of the large numbers of young people who leave school with written language problems, some (including many undiagnosed children with dyslexia) undoubtedly should have received different rather than more of the traditional remedial approaches.

For an even larger number of students, the major problem which hinders them from achieving their reading potential continues to be one of resources, that is, too few adequately qualified teachers with sufficient time to deliver their skills.

There is a considerable overlap between the needs of children with dyslexia and other special needs children. They require teaching that is structured, sequential, cumulative and thorough - a British Dyslexia Association recommendation, and invariably are demanding of teacher time.

Some systems that meet these characteristics can be challenging to teachers. They often require a large amount of overlearning which often elicits the criticism of their being boring. But that they sometimes work when all else fails is justification enough.

A key issue is, whether the considerable range of teaching/learning methods, techniques and materials currently available are differentially effective with pupils having identifiably different learning characteristics. Pumfrey and Reason (1991) put forward some 20 specialized approaches with the caveat that the differential efficacies of the methods and materials are not unequivocally established.

The considerable range of teaching/learning techniques and material currently available all come with guarantees. Some are research based but others have been the fruits of '...work by gifted individuals who were influenced little or not all by the findings of experimental psychologists' (Miles & Ellis, 1981). Experience suggests the latter often prove easier to assimilate into normal classroom practice and consequently have the potential to be more effective instruments of change.

The majority of the specialized approaches which are said to be effective in teaching those with dyslexia have concentrated upon phonic skills. But successes have been claimed with other approaches that have concentrated upon building upon strengths, such as visual and semantic aspects of language, rather than attempts to correct weaknesses. Ideally, individualized programmes should aim to identify and improve a pupil's relatively weak information processing skills and capitalize on alternative strategies and strengths where possible.

Multi-sensory approaches have appeal. They provide a catch-all system which can prove effective for undifferentiate dyslexics. Specific approaches may prove to be more efficient for particular sub-types.

Many children with a history of learning failure require and benefit from the discipline provided by 'precision teaching'. Precision teaching is not a new method or technique of teaching. It is a system which focuses attention on the planning and monitoring of any teaching method or technique.

Precision teaching

- is not a method of teaching but a way of trying to find out 'what teaches best';
- is a precise means of describing pupils' educational performance;
- is a means of measuring progress on a direct and regular (daily) basis;
- uses techniques for keeping daily records, including graphic displays, of pupils' progress;
- provides guidelines for making changes in the teaching programmes.

For teachers to use precision teaching successfully they need to be aware of the various teaching methods, approaches and materials that are available. No one path to achieving proficiency in written language skills is likely to be taken by all pupils. Circuitous routes are required for some children who have great difficulty in reaching their goal of literacy and numeracy.

Precision teaching uses behavioural principles to enable changes in pupils' performance to be observed and measured. It does not necessitate the use of behavioural teaching techniques but allows for a wide range of intervention strategies.

Other techniques

Although a great many factors may contribute to children's difficulties in learning not all will be amenable to change. The majority will respond to the some combination of the three most direct strategies open to teachers.

1. Change the task

Task analysis may result in a need for a reduction in the size of task requirements, 'task slicing', or breaking down the current teaching objectives into a series of intermediate objectives.

2. Change the teaching approach

Changes of the teacher's management of the pupil or of the method of teaching or the materials may be required.

3. Improve motivation

When individualized programmes fail to induce enthusiasm some form of contingency contracting may be required.

Using Parents: Paired Reading

Another approach towards helping children with severe written language difficulties, including those diagnosed as having dyslexia, is by using the still undervalued resource of energy and goodwill of parents. The role of parents as partners in meeting the needs of children with difficulties is now firmly established but continues to be under-used by teachers.

Research carried out by Young and Tyre (1983) showed that parents were the major contributors in the success their children achieved. An important element of their contribution, and one which has continued to prove successful with many parents of poor readers since, was the use of the 'paired reading technique'. In the aforementioned research, parents were asked to work with their children for fifteen minutes per day at a reading session where they followed a set procedure.

Having first read the passage, the parent then:

- talks about the passage, the pictures, characters, the story so far, with the child, for two or three minutes;
- reads the passage aloud as naturally and with as much expression as possible, while running a finger along under the lines of print, for three minutes;
- reads the passage aloud with the child joining in, in unison, i.e. paired reading, for three minutes;
- reads the passage aloud with the child in unison, but this time pausing occasionally for the child to provide the next word or phrase at points in the text

where the parent is reasonably certain the child will be able to carry on - three minutes;

- lets the child read the passage aloud. Should the child hesitate the parent supplies the word or phrase - three minutes.

A complete description of the parental contribution is in Young and Tyre (1983). Many methods are proposed for the remediation of dyslexia that have not been established to be effective using well-controlled studies. Parents and teachers should be careful in purchasing expensive equipment or programmes which have not been adequately researched and tested.

References

Bakker, D. J. & Vinke, J. (1985) Effects of Hemisphere - Specific Stimulation on Brain Activity and Reading in Dyslexics. *Journal of Clinical and Experimental Neuropsychology* 1985 pp 505-525.

Bakker, D.J. (1990) *Neuropsychological Treatments of Dyslexia*. Oxford University Press. Oxford.

Bradley, L. (1984) *Assessing Reading Difficulties; A Diagnostic and Remedial Approach*. Macmillan. London.

Bradley, L. & Bryant, P. (1985) *Rhyme and Reason in Reading and Spelling*. Ann Arbor. University of Michigan Press.

Bullock, Sir A. (1975) *A Language for Life, The Bullock Report*. H.M.S.O. London.

Chasty, H. & Friel, J. (1991) *Children with Special Needs*. Jessica Kingsley Publishers. London.

Chomsky, N.C. (1976) Approaching Reading through Invented Spelling in Resnick, L.B. & Weaver, P.A. (Eds.) *Theory and Practice of Early Reading*. Erlbaum. Hillsdale, New York.

Clark, M. (1970) *Reading Difficulties in Schools*. Penguin Books. Harmondsworth.

Coltheart, M. Patterson & Marshall, J. (1980) *Deep Dyslexia*. Routledge & Kegan Paul. London.

Critchley, M. (1970) The Dyslexic Child. Thomas. Springfield, Illinois.

Elliott, C. (1990) The Definition and Identification of Specific Learning Difficulties in Pumfrey, P. and Elliott, C. *Children's Difficulties in Reading, Spelling and Writing*. (Eds.) Falmer Press. Basingstoke.

Farnham-Diggory, S. (1978) *Learning Disabilities*. Fontana/Open Books. London.

Huey, E. (1980) *The Psychology and Pedagogy of Reading*. Macmillan. New York. (Republished by MIT Press. Cambridge, Mass. 1968.)

Iredell, H. (1988) Eleanor Learns to Read. *Education* 19. pp 233-8.

Masland, R. (1990) Neurological Aspects of Dyslexia in Hales, G. (Editor) *Meeting Points in Dyslexia*. British Dyslexia Association.

Maxwell, J. (1977) *Reading Progress from 8-15*. NFER Publishing. Slough.

Melnick, A. & Merritt, J. (1972) *Reading Today and Tomorrow*. OUP. London.

Miles, T. & Ellis, N. (1981) A Lexical Coding Deficiency II in Paylidis, G. & Miles, T. (Eds.) *Dyslexia Research and its Application to Education*. Wiley. Chichester.

Mortimore, P., Sammons, P., Stoll, P., Lewis, D. & Ecob, R. (1988) *School Matters*. Open Books. London.

Moss, G. (1996) Quality for All. *Special Children* Issue 92 pp 53-59. Questions Publishing Company. Birmingham.

Neisser, U. (1967) *Cognitive Psychology*. Appleton Earlbaum Crofts. New York.

Orton, S. (1925) Word Blindness in School Children. *Archives of Neurology and Psychiatry*. 14:581-615.

Pavlidis, G.T. (1985) Eye Movements in Dyslexia: Their Diagnostic Significance. *Journal of Learning Disabilities*, 18, pp 42-50.

Pumfrey, P. (1985) *Reading: Tests and Assessment Techniques (2nd Ed.)* Hodder and Stoughton in association with the UKRA. London.

Pumfrey, P. & Reason, R. (1991) *Specific Learning Difficulties*. NFER Nelson. Windsor.

Rutter, M., Maugham, B. & Ouston, J. (1979) *Fifteen Thousand Hours: Secondary Schools and their Effects on Children*. Open Books. London.

Rutter, M., Tizzard, J. & Whitmore, K. (1970) *Education Health and Behaviour*. Longman. London.

Shallice, T. & Warrington, E. (1980) Single and Multiple Component Central Dyslexic Syndromes in Coltheart et al (Editors) *Deep Dyslexia*. Routledge and Kegan Paul. London.

Smith, F. (1978) *Reading*. Cambridge University Press. Cambridge.

Southgate, V., Arnold, H. & Johnson, S. (1981) *Extending Beginning Reading*. Heinemann Educational Books for the Schools Council.

Springer, S.P. & Deutch (1989) *Left Brain, Right Brain* (3rd edition). W.H. Freeman & Company. New York.

Tansley, P. & Pankhurst, J. (1981) *Children with Specific Learning Difficulties*. NFER Nelson. Windsor.

Turner, M. (1988) *Teaching Reading - Uplift and After - Theoretical Critique of Emergent Identification*. EPIX Communication.

Young, P. & Tyre, C. (1983) *Dyslexia or Illiteracy*. Open University Press. Milton Keynes.

Young, P. & Tyre, C. (1985) *Teach Your Child to Read*. Fontana Paperback. London.

Whittington, J. & Richards, P. (1987) The stability of children's laterality prevalences and their relationship to measures of performance. *British Journal of Educational Psychology* 57, 45-55.

Suggested Reading

Bryant, P. & Bradley, L. (1985) *Children's Reading Problems*. Basil Blackwell Ltd. Oxford.

Crystal, D. (1987) *The Cambridge Encyclopaedia of Language*. Cambridge University Press. Cambridge.

Goswami, U. & Bryant, P. (1990) *Phonological Skills and Learning to Read*. Lawrence Erlbaum Associates Ltd. Hove.

Pumfrey, P. & Reason, R. (1991) *Specific Learning Difficulties*. NFER Nelson. Windsor.

Reason, R. & Boote, R. (1994) *Helping Children with Reading and Spelling - A Special Needs Manual*. Routledge. London.

Singleton, C. (1994) *Computers and Dyslexia*. The Dyslexia Computer Resource Centre, Department of Psychology, Hull HU6 7RX.

Snowling, M. (1985) *Children's Written Language Difficulties*. NFER Nelson. Windsor.

Underwood, G. and Batt, V. (1996) *Reading and Understanding*. Blackwell. Oxford.

Webster, A., Beveridge, M. & Reed, M. (1996) *Managing the Literacy Curriculum*. Routledge. London.

Young, P. & Tyre, C. (1983) *Dyslexia or Illiteracy*. Open University Press. Milton Keynes.

Young, P. & Tyre, C. (1985) *Teach Your Child to Read*. Fontana Paperbacks. London.

YOUNG & TYRE (1985) consider lessons that children learn about print in the lap-learning stage essential components in the apprenticeship to reading.

1. Reading is enjoyable, useful and a way of communicating.

2. You can represent things which you have in your head, in colours and shape on paper.

3. Pictures mean more or less the same thing to everyone. They can be discussed.

4. Reading has meaning, just like speech.

5. Printed language describes things so clearly they can be easily imagined.

6. Books open from left to right.

7. Print usually goes from the top left to the bottom right on each page.

8. You can read aloud or to yourself.

9. You can act on what you read.

10. Print in books is like print in the street or around the house.

11. You can copy letters or words.

Principles for Learning to Read

1. Create appreciation for the written word.

2. Develop awareness of printed language.

3. Teach the alphabet.

4. Develop phonemic analysis.

5. Teach the relation of sounds and letters.

6. Teach children how to sound out words.

7. Teach children to spell words.

8. Help children develop fluent, reflective reading.

For Chomsky (1976) the discovery approach purports that children can and should *write first* and *read later.*

1. The teacher's message to the children with regard to spelling is that their judgement is good, trust it and figure out how the word sounds and write it down that way.

2. A bucketful of letters, a diary and reason for writing are provided.

3. A great deal of time is spent reading stories and discussing the words in the stories.

4. The children work on beginning sounds, end sounds and rhymes.

5. They work on the idea of sequence in words. Children's names are used for this.

6. They are given reason for writing.

7. Using plastic letters frees some children who have handwriting problems in the early stages.

8. When children write, they read what they write.

9. The children are expected to write from the start.

FROM LAP LEARNING TO LITERACY

9 months	**Pointing at things** **Pointing at pictures** **Rag and Board books**
12 months	**Picture books** **Picture story books** **Picture alphabet books** **Picture and word books** **Story books with pictures**
3 years	**Shared reading** **Shared reading games**
4 years	**Paired reading** **Paired reading games**
6 years	**Prepared reading - reading to learn**
7 years	**Guided reading** **Study methods**
10 years	**Independent study** **Discriminatory reading** **Critical reading**

Young and Tyre (1985)

EFFECTIVE TEACHING OF READING REQUIRES

- **A knowledge of basic processes involved**

- **The use of a model of reading which allows for teaching methods to be justified**

- **The use of a model of reading which allows for learning difficulties and errors to be understood**

- **The use of a model to give direction to planning effective treatment programmes**

A History Lesson for the Minister of Education

1861	A Government Commission reported that standards were too low. It recommended that funding should be based on performance.
1884	A Royal Commission of Enquiry found that German education was superior to Britain's.
1885	A Commission of Enquiry found that payment by results led to falling standards.
1912	The 'Times' commented that most people - even educated ones - couldn't spell. It reported comments from a headteacher that reading standards were falling because parents no longer read to their children and that too much time was spent listening to the gramophone.
1913	Employers complained that school leavers were poor in spelling, grammar and calculating.
1921	The Newbold Report said that pupils could not spell or punctuate.
1925	School Inspectors reported that pupils were 'far inferior to the previous generation'.
1938	The Spens Report found that 'many pupils pass through grammar school, and even university, without acquiring the capacity to express themselves in English'.
1943	The Norwood Report pointed to falling standards in English and blamed the schools.
1969	The first Black Paper complained of falling standards in spelling, reading, writing and mathematics and blamed comprehensive schools.
1996	Poor standards of literacy, numeracy and teaching remain the three problem areas in education, according to HM Chief Inspector. English and maths were highlighted as the worst areas, particularly at KS2, where only three-quarters of lessons were well taught. (OFSTED)

THE READING BRAIN

- **Rapid early development**

- **The early stages of growth are arguably the most important (if not critical) for healthy development**

- **Cerebral lateralization**

- **Cerebral localization**

- **Areas associated with speaking, reading, writing**

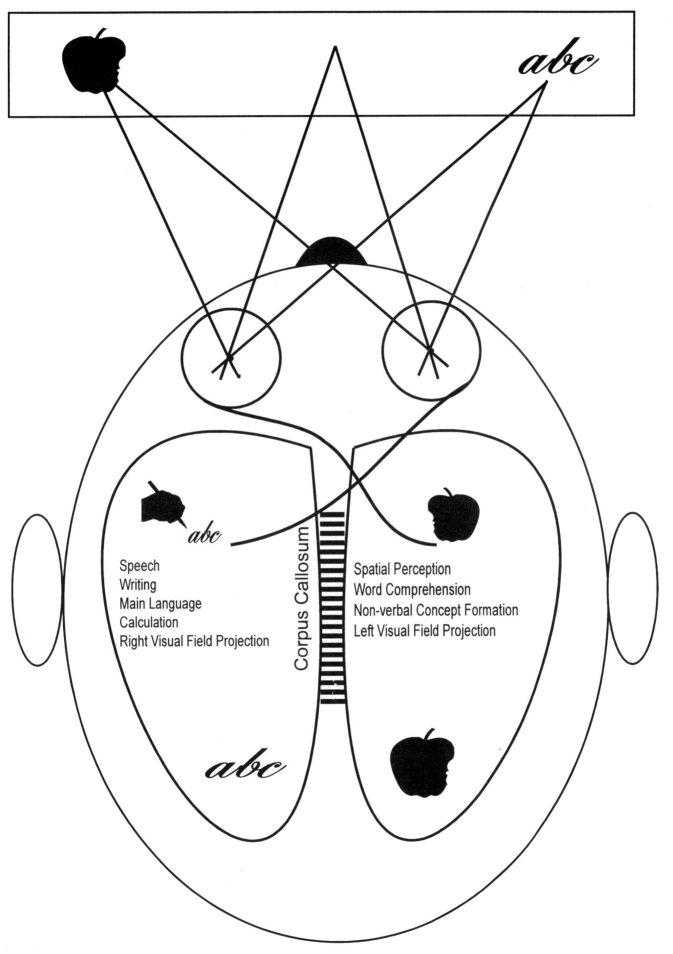

- Poorly developed laterality and reading-deficit could both be due to the effects of an actual cerebral lesion.

- Reading-deficit and lack of cerebral asymmetry could both be taken as evidence of a constitutional maturational lag.

- Children who lack firm lateral preferences also happen to be particularly vulnerable to stress.

Zangwill (1962)

We know only five things for sure:

1. It is possible for one hemisphere to take control of a simple task that is presented - through the ears, eyes or hands - to both hemispheres at once.

2. These dominance effects may change with development.

3. The effects may not be the same for males and females.

4. They may not be the same for dyslexic and normal children.

5. They may shift as a function of learning sets induced by certain forms of school instruction.

Learning disabilities may occur in three different areas

1. There may be a problem in moving information from one hemisphere to another.

2. There may be a task-specific problem with one of the hemispheres so that it performs inadequately when it takes its turn.

3. There may be a task-specific problem of overall control by the left hemisphere.

Writing a Word

		Hemisphere
1. Bring the sound of the word to mind.		**Left**
2. Select a sound particle.		**Left**
3. Match a letter pattern in the memory.		**Right**
4. Write the letters.	**Right for the configuration of letters**	**Left for the motor action**
5. Check the letter pattern.		**Right**
6. Test the finished word.		**Right**

SOME OF THE NEURAL PATHWAYS CONSIDERED TO BE INVOLVED IN THE PROCESSING OF SPOKEN LANGUAGE

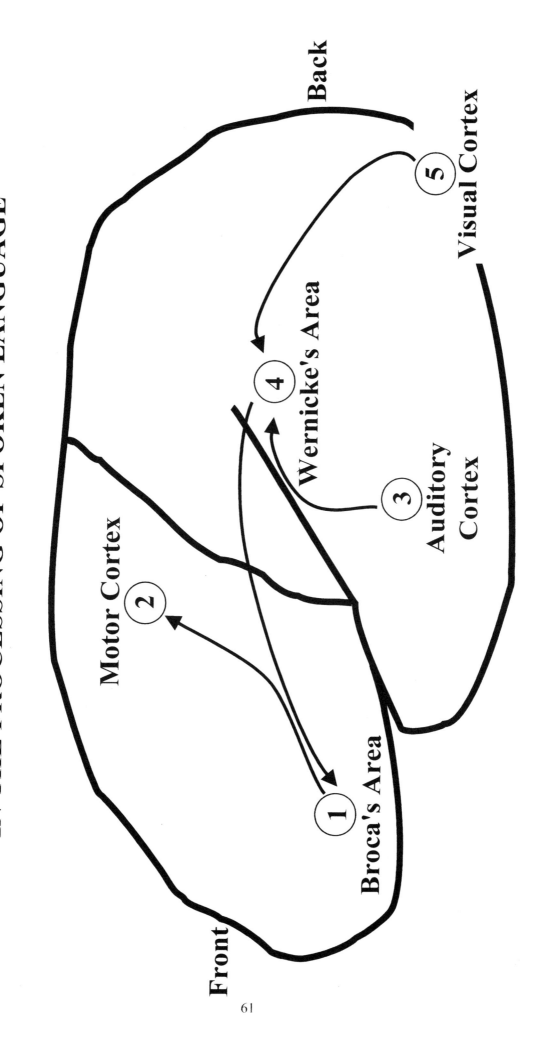

THE PROCESS OF READING ALOUD INVOLVES

- the VISUAL CORTEX (5) which

- activates the WERNICKE'S AREA (4)

- associated auditory representations from the AUDITORY CORTEX (3)

- stimulation in the Wernicke's Area is transmitted to the BROCA'S AREA (1) for encoding

- the coded programmes are then passed on to the adjacent MOTOR AREA (2) which governs the articulatory response

THE READING PROCESS

'Reading, whether it is defined as literacy, language, arts, English, Dyslexia or backwardness - is the subject of concerned discussion and divisive debate in communities and their legislative bodies, in business and in industry, in academic institutions and professional organisations, as well as among theorists and practitioners'

Melnick & Merritt, 1972

Reading involves abilities to

Decode - Gain Lexical Access - Organize Text

Reading Models

Analytic (Bottom-Up)

The strength of direct evidence coming largely from the analyses of stimulus input or bottom-up processing, and

Constructivist (Top-Down)

The contextual support coming from the same and higher levels, indicating the amount of top-down support.

Interactive/Rumelhart

Total strengths = the combined relationship of feature and contextual based components.

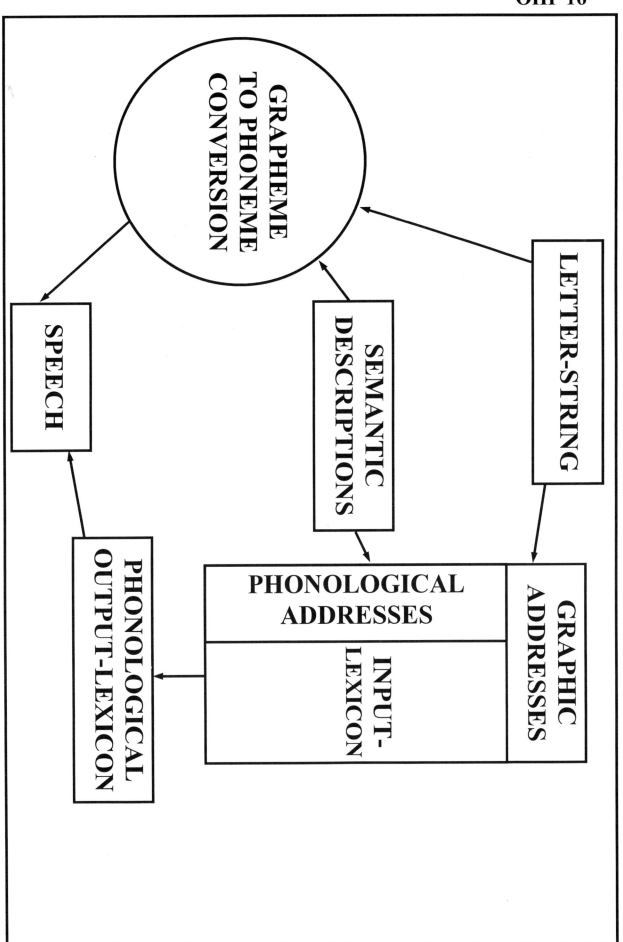

INDIVIDUAL DIFFERENCES IN READING

- For the majority of children, written language skills appear to be acquired more or less adequately irrespective of what method or teaching approach is used.

- If individual differences in reading are on a continuum of reading ability then the same forces affect poor readers alike. What is good for one is good for all.

- If, however, the forces which stand in the way are peculiar to them, then it is necessary to differentiate teaching systems, methods and materials. Different difficulties usually require different remedies.

FIELD-DEPENDENT/INDEPENDENT COGNITIVE STYLE

Poor readers (generally field-dependent):

- do less reading

- read more orally than silently

- get interrupted more often by the teacher for errors

- get more instructional focus on decoding, as opposed to comprehension

FIELD-DEPENDENT READERS

- fail to effectively utilize appropriate and available prior knowledge in reading for comprehension

- may select inappropriate prior knowledge schema

- ineffectively use text-based cues

- inflexibly maintain inappropriate schema when reading

- allocate attention inappropriately thereby missing critical information and cues

POOR READERS NEED

- help in paying attention to meaning

- help in using less obvious meaning and contextual cues

- to be encouraged to make meaningful predictions about whole texts

- reading material that deals with social situations

- structural support, e.g. purpose-setting content webs and teacher outlines

TYPES OF DYSLEXIA

- ACQUIRED DYSLEXIA

- DEEP DYSLEXIA

- PHONOLOGICAL DYSLEXIA

- SURFACE DYSLEXIA

- HYPERLEXIA

- DEVELOPMENTAL DYSLEXIA

DEVELOPMENTAL DYSLEXIA
Some possible causes and effects

- Dominance and Laterality
- Cerebral Dominance
- Localization
- Visual Skills
    - Tracking
    - Visual Scan
    - Saccadic Eye Movements
- Scotopic Sensitivity
- Emotional & Behavioural Difficulties
- Self-concept and Motivation
- Environmental Correlates
- Cognitive Aspects
    - phonemic awareness
    - phonemic segmentation
    - naming difficulties
    - lexical retrieval
    - early rhyming ability
    - short term memory span (auditory, visual)
    - speed of processing
    - sequencing difficulties
    - clumsiness
    - genetics
    - drugs

VISUAL SCAN

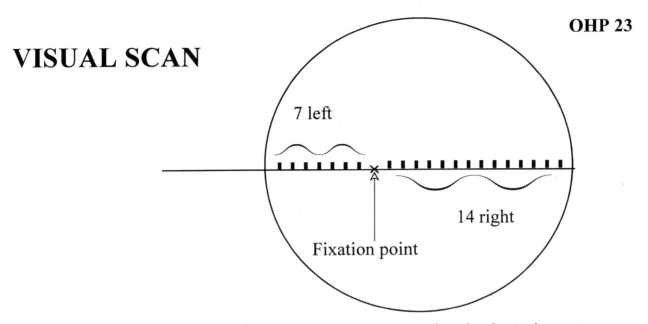

Competent readers have an asymmetrical visual scan taking in about 14 characters to the right and about 7 to the left

SACCADIC EYE MOVEMENTS

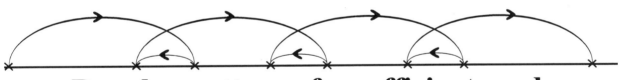

Regular pattern of an efficient reader

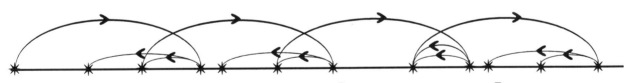

Irregular pattern of a poor reader

Reading eye movements of children with dyslexia differ from those of normal readers.

×   Short fixation points
✻   Long fixation and more regression

STRATEGY FOR THE IDENTIFICATION OF DYSLEXIA

- Governors and staff are aware of educational needs of pupils

- Clear school procedure for identification

- Monitoring of programmes

- Systematic recording

- All adults are aware of pupils' educational needs

- School publishes policy